FRANCES GARDNER HUNTER

is the bestselling author of HOT LINE TO HEAVEN and GOD IS FABULOUS! A successful Miami businesswoman, she is the mother of a teenaged daughter and a married son. Mrs. Hunter, a well-known public speaker, is also founder of the Christian Youth Movement, Alpha/Omega, and an active contributor to Campus Crusade for Christ and the Sunland Youth Center in Miami.

GO, MAN, GO! is her direct and often humorous story of witnessing for Christ, and the frustrations and fulfillments of that often misunderstood calling. In any language, Frances Gardner Hunter is a rarity: a joyous, sharing, alive human being who is herself one of the best advertisements for Christian faith, hope, and charity.

GO, MAN, GO!

FRANCES GARDNER HUNTER

WARNER PRESS Anderson, Indiana

GO, MAN, GO!

A PORTAL BOOK
Published by Pyramid Publications for Warner Press, Inc.

Third printing, February 1972

Printed in the United States of America

PORTAL BOOKS are published by Warner Press, Inc.
1200 East 5th Street, Anderson, Indiana 46011, U.S.A.

CONTENTS

CHAPTER 1

WITNESSING IS FABULOUS!

And Jesus came and spake unto them, saying, All power is given unto me in heaven and in earth. Go ye therefore, and teach all nations. . . .—Matthew 28:18-19a

THE MOST EXCITING chapter in the entire Bible is the 29th chapter of Acts . . . and if you don't believe it, try it! It's exciting because it's the chapter that you and I are privileged to write. So don't try finding it in the Bible, because it's not complete yet, but *do try writing your share of this new chapter.*

9

Go, Man, Go!

I like the shortest verse in the Bible. Many people think it's the verse which says: "Jesus wept," but in my version, the shortest verse has just one word, and that is the word "Go." People tell me there's more to the verse than just that one word, but if there is, the first word says so much to me that I haven't read the rest of it, but have only obeyed the command given in the first word of that Great Commission.

Somehow or other I'm on a spiritual cloud or a mountaintop most of the time. And I hope that from this book you might learn a little of the reason why I stay on the mountaintop. (And it isn't because my own life doesn't have problems, either.)

Following that one little word "Go" has led me into some of the most fantastic situations, but believing that "wherever I go, God goes with me, and that makes me a majority" lets me come out on top and has given me an exciting, adventuresome life I wouldn't trade with any-one.

I have heard probably every excuse in the book as to why people can't witness, and if you have made any of them, be prepared to have a knife stuck in you through the pages of this book (or throw the book away right now), because that's probably what I'll do (in a Christian way, of course).

I've read the Bible forward, backward, upside down, and I can't find anything in it which gives any physical specifications for being a witness for Christ. I can't find anything in the Bible which says you have to be beautiful, young, educated, possessed of great gifts of oratory, or any other attribute to obey the Great Commission.

Christ didn't tell me I had to be a "knock-out" (it's a good thing). He didn't tell me I had to be the greatest theologian in the world (that's a good thing, too). He

10

didn't tell me I had to be the smartest person in the world (and that's *really* a good thing). He didn't tell me I had to be the cleverest person in the world (He must have known I'd come along and hear his call). But he very simply said to me, "Go tell everybody." He didn't say I had to be a real genius and figure out all kinds of schemes and ways to be able to talk to people; he just said in great love to "tell everybody."

And what do I tell everybody? Just the very simple story of Jesus. Here is a man who lived such a perfectly simple, uncomplicated life, and whose only claim to fame was the "greatest story ever told." Here is a man who died for people like you and me, a man who gave his life in a horrible, agonizing death that you and I might be saved from sin and have eternal life. If he was willing to do this for us, why don't we all do just one little thing for him: "go tell everybody"? He promised us an "abundant" life, and how can we expect to claim his promise if we don't do the one little thing he asks us to do?

I hear people talk about their new cars: how many colors they come in; how many miles the tires are guaranteed for; how many gadgets are on the car; how long the car will last; how comfortable it is; how much it costs, or how little (not today they don't); and I wonder why they can't talk in the same way about something far more exciting than a car.

If you will think about Christ as a car, this is what you might come up with: a "new" car—Christ is new to anyone who hasn't heard the gospel and he's new to me every day because of the things he reveals to me daily since he gave me a "new" life. And talk about *power!* You don't even know what power is until you know the power of the Holy Spirit. How fast can you go? Only as fast or as slow as you want to go because Christ never forces himself upon you. How many colors?

Christ isn't reserved for any one color. He belongs to all. How many miles is he guaranteed for? He's guaranteed for a lifetime, not just for a few miles. How many gadgets are on the car? Well, figure gadgets as blessings, and see how many Christ can give you. How long will Christ last? For all eternity. How much does Christ cost? He's a free gift—no payments to make, no taxes to pay, no mortgages to worry about, but an exciting gift to enjoy through all eternity. Now isn't that a lot more exciting than talking about a car?

And I hear women swapping recipes, discussing the high price of food at the store, and all sorts of things that many times neither of them are interested in discussing, but it's "something to talk about." And yet think how much more fun it is to swap recipes on how to lead someone to a personal relationship with Christ. Think of the low cost of saving someone's soul, because of the high price that Someone paid for us.

So many people who hang on the brink of Christianity, do so because they're afraid to try giving Christ away, and yet this will bring a joy that nothing else can.

There is a little secret, though, and before I tell you about the different kinds of witnessing, I want to ask you one question. Do *you* really know Christ? (Well, there went that knife!) If you're not sure, then here's your second chance to throw the book away. If you're still hanging on, then your desire must be right, but maybe you need just a little help.

All that God wants from me is to be able to use me as an instrument for his work. This was probably the most difficult thing for me to learn as an overzealous, stupid, new Christian. I really wanted to go out and turn the whole world upside down for Christ, all by myself. And I found out that I surely couldn't do it all by myself, but that if I would just relax a little more and be tuned in on station GOD all the time, he would use me in a fabulous way.

The Holy Spirit is the secret of witnessing, and I hope you don't get trapped by people saying "successful witnessing." Let me assure you that any sincere witnessing is "successful," because Christ just commanded us to sow the seeds, and we must remember there is *nothing* we can do to add anyone to God's kingdom. That's a privilege he reserves for himself.

Did you ever see a tiger rug? You know, the kind that lies on the floor flatter than a pancake but with mouth wide open and teeth showing? That's what I feel like every time I've tried to go out witnessing on my own. I fall so flat on my face it's revolting, and I feel exactly like the tiger rug looks spread out all over the floor.

It's easy to witness, actually, if you'll just "go along for the ride." Keeping yourself submerged and letting God use you can make it really easy for you, and really exciting as well, and what a blessing an instrument of God can be to someone else.

Warning: Second knifing coming up! If you're still with me, ask yourself honestly: "Am I filled with the Holy Spirit?" Are you sure? If not, claim the promise of Christ and ask to be filled with the Holy Spirit *right now!* And I hope you'll say "thank you." People often think the universe will collapse when they're filled with the Holy Spirit, the thunder will roll, the lightning will strike, and when they don't hear any of this they think they're not filled with the Holy Spirit. But Christ doesn't lie and he fulfills his promises today just as he always

13

has, so ask him to fill you . . . and he will! Just that simple! But don't be "saved and sanctified" for sixty years and then say the only thing the Lord ever gave you was arthritis! (One lady *did* say that.)

If you've survived the two knifings to date, I'd just like to tell you that some of the incidents I'll be sharing with you in this book are successful, some of you may think some of them are not, but regardless of the outcome I have done what Christ commanded: I have "gone."

Mark 12:30, 31 says: " 'and you shall love the Lord your God with all your heart, and with all your soul, and with all your mind, and with all your strength.' The second is this, 'You shall love your neighbor as yourself.' There is *no other commandment* greater than these."

If you really stop to analyze these two verses you know that Jesus said we have to love God with everything we possess. If we love God this way, what can we do other than what he wants us to do? Because when we love someone, don't we do everything we can to please that one?

Remember when you fell in love? If you're a man, I can imagine all the things you did to please your loved one. You probably brought her a red rose as a romantic gesture; you probably wrote her poetry; you probably would have stood on your head if she had asked you! In other words, you did everything in your power to please her because you loved her.

If you're a woman, you probably learned all the female tricks he enjoyed, and used them all on him. (I know, because I did, too.) Didn't you do all the things you could think of to please him because you were sooooo in love? That's all that God asks out of us:

enough love to have a desire to please him and do his will.

Think of verse 31: "You shall love your neighbor as yourself." Suppose you have an unchristian neighbor. If he died tonight, where would he be? You know the answer, don't you? He'd be in hell! Now if you love him as yourself, that means you want to go to hell, too! Think about all the people you came in contact with today—do you honestly *love them as yourself?*

If the love of God shines through you, how could you ever not want to share the exciting story of Jesus Christ? If you really want something to make you think, make up a little chart and at the top put two headings, "Saved" and "Lost," and then underneath them write the names of all your friends and loved ones and put a check mark in the column which you think applies to each of them. Does it bother you when you put a check mark under "Lost"? It ought to!

All right, where do we go from here? Pray, and I mean really pray with your heart and soul, asking God to use you and give you courage, because until you've really gotten over that first hurdle, you can really be scared. Prayer is really a fabulous thing when you pray in faith, believing! The first time I ever went witnessing I was scared speechless (and for me that's a neat trick).

Ed Waxer of Campus Crusade for Christ introduced me to the "Four Spiritual Laws" which are reproduced with the permission of Campus Crusade for Christ; and if you can't do anything else, you can just read word for word what it says on the pages of the booklet.

And if you're scared, don't worry! I was so scared the first time I went out to witness I almost became unglued. I prayed so hard that no one would be home. I think I must have even prayed that I would get sick

Just as there are physical laws that govern the physical universe, so there are spiritual laws which govern your relationship with God.

LAW ONE

GOD **LOVES** YOU, AND HAS A WONDERFUL PLAN FOR YOUR LIFE.

(Scripture references contained in this booklet should be read in context from the Bible wherever possible.)

GOD'S LOVE
John 3:16 "For God so loved the world, that He gave His only begotten Son, that whosoever believeth in Him should not perish, but have everlasting life."

GOD'S PLAN
John 10:10b (Christ speaking) "I am come that they might have life, and that they might have it more abundantly" (A full and meaningful life).

Why is it that most people are not experiencing the abundant life?

Because

LAW TWO

MAN IS **SINFUL** AND **SEPARATED** FROM GOD, THUS HE CANNOT KNOW AND EXPERIENCE GOD'S LOVE AND PLAN FOR HIS LIFE.

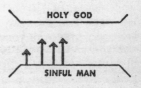

(Man is continually trying to reach God and the abundant life through his own efforts, good life, ethics, philosophy, etc.)

MAN IS SINFUL
Romans 3:23 "For all have sinned and come short of the glory of God."
(Sin is an attitude of indifference to God, and is characterized by an attitude of active or passive rebellion.)

MAN IS SEPARATED
Romans 6:23 "For the wages of sin is death . . ."
(Man was created to have fellowship with God, but because of his own stubborn self-will, man chose to go his own independent way and fellowship with God was broken.)

The Third Law gives us the only answer to this dilemma.

LAW THREE

JESUS CHRIST IS GOD'S **ONLY** PROVISION FOR MAN'S SIN. THROUGH HIM YOU CAN KNOW GOD'S LOVE AND PLAN FOR YOUR LIFE.

God seeking man

Romans 5:8
"But God proves His love for us, in that while we were yet sinners, Christ died for us."

John 14:6
"Jesus saith unto him, I am the way, the truth, and the life: no man cometh unto the Father, but by me."

II Corinthians 5:21
"For He (God) hath made Him (Christ) to be sin for us, who (Christ) knew no sin: that we might be made the righteousness of God in Him."

It is not enough to know these three laws or even to believe them . .

LAW FOUR

WE MUST **RECEIVE** JESUS CHRIST AS SAVIOR AND LORD BY **PERSONAL INVITATION.**

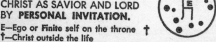

E—Ego or **Finite** self on the throne †
†—Christ outside the life
●—Interests controlled by self resulting in discord and frustration
†—Christ in the life
●—Interests under control of **Infinite** God, resulting in harmony and purpose.

HOW TO RECEIVE CHRIST: (Read John 3:1-8)

John 1:12 "But as many as **received** Him, to them gave He power to become the sons of God, even to them that believe in His name."

PERSONAL INVITATION

Revelation 3:20 (Christ is speaking) "Behold I stand at the door and knock: If any man hear my voice, and open the door, **I will come in to him** . . ."

"Receiving" Christ involves commitment of the total person—intellect, emotion and will. (The change which follows this initial act may be sudden or gradual according to one's personality.)

Is there any good reason why you wouldn't like to **receive** Christ right now?

right on the spot so I wouldn't have to go into a house. I prayed every ridiculous prayer in the world, and yet I obeyed Christ's command to "GO" regardless of how frightened I was. He honored my obedience and gave me one of the most exciting days of my life and started me on the most exciting thing in the Christian life: witnessing!

Come with me, won't you, as I take you on some witnessing adventures with me. And witnessing is always an *adventure!*

CHAPTER 2

WHAT KIND ARE YOU?

. . . Jesus suffered him not, but saith unto him, Go home to thy friends, and tell them how great things the Lord hath done for thee, and hath had compassion on thee. And he departed, and began to publish in Decapolis how great things Jesus had done for him, and all men did marvel.—Mark 5:19-20

DO YOU REMEMBER the first time you heard the word "witness" used in church? I do. I remember thinking there must have been an accident or something and someone needed some witnesses. I wasn't going to get involved in any kind of lawsuit or anything like that, no siree!

It was my first time attending the evening service of my church and the pastor asked for a "testimony" and I knew immediately they were involved in some kind of legal hassle where they needed witnesses to testify. I thought it must be something awful because it seemed like nobody wanted to speak, but finally a woman got up and made a very simple statement, "I want to thank the Lord for saving my soul!" And then she sat down, and I wondered what kind of witness this was, and yet I think today what an exciting witness she was.

She was an elderly lady, had been a Christian many, many years through trials and tribulations. She loved Jesus with a passion and a faithfulness found in few people today. When I met her she was no longer "active" in church because she was physically unable, but she played a great part in our church's growth for just one simple little fact. (God rest her soul . . . she went to join him a year or so ago.) I'll always remember her as an exciting witness for Christ because she was "always there."

If it was Sunday school, Mollie was there.

If it was morning worship, Mollie was there.

If it was evening worship, Mollie was there.

If it was a business meeting, Mollie was there.

If it was a church picnic, Mollie was there.

If it was a church play, Mollie was there.

And as I began attending all the church services myself, after such an exciting introduction to Christ, I found myself looking for her, and when I saw Mollie in her familiar place, there was a calm feeling that all was right with the world and the service could begin. I wasn't privileged to know her really well, and I wasn't privileged to know her when she was "active" in the church, but I was privileged to see the contribution she made by just "being there."

I looked up the word "witness" in Webster's dictionary and as a noun, the following definition is given:

> "testimony; attestation of a fact or event; evidence; a person who saw, or who can give a firsthand account of, something; . . . something providing or serving as evidence; to bear witness; to *be,* or *give* evidence."

Mollie really proved the definition to be a real fact because her very presence was "attestation of a fact or event; evidence." Insofar as being a "person who saw, or who can give a firsthand account of, something," she certainly was able to give a firsthand account of knowing Christ in a personal way; "something providing or serving as evidence"; she certainly served as evidence because she was "there"; "to *be,* or *give* evidence," Mollie not only *was* evidence, she *gave* evidence. She gave evidence that Christ came first in her life, because she never put anything else in front of him. A few years ago I might not have been able to understand Mollie's being a witness, but today I can see she was a very special kind of witness.

THE ROBOT WITNESS

I'm going to try and share with you all the possible and impossible kinds of witnessing I can think of in the hope that somewhere along the line you will find the niche where you belong as a witness. Not very long ago, Alpha/Omega, the Christian Youth Movement I started in 1966, was out on one of the beaches in Miami sharing the excitement of Christ with other people on the beach.

My church had loaned a bus for the young people to go out in. And it is one of the usual church monstrosities: painted that horrible yellow with the name emblazoned in big—bold—black letters on the side: . . . CHURCH.

Somehow it seems to me that few churches can afford streamlined, modern buses painted a luxurious pale blue with lots of shiny chrome, and all kinds of air conditioning, automatic windows, and such. Most seem to go the hard route and advertise Christ in a worn out "chug-chug" type of thing that puffs and pants whenever there is the slightest incline, and the kind of thing where you'd better pray there's a chiropractor in the congregation (P.T.L. we have one in ours) . . . so he can get the kinks out of your back when you get back (*if* you get back).

And things always happen, like the night the clutch fell out on the highway. Can you imagine the exciting "witness" we were with a busload of teen-age kids and the clutch lying on the highway? Well, I had never thought of any church bus as being a very exciting witness for Christ. They sway and tip dangerously with reckless abandon as they carry singing teen-agers on jaunts for Jesus. Then came the day the kids returned and told me how our church bus had "witnessed."

It seems that when they got to the beach the group had split up into two's and three's to search out individuals who needed Christ. A team came upon a lady who was sitting in the sand and who looked like she was either digging castles in the sand or burying something!

They started talking to her, and before long she admitted to a great need in her life to know Christ better.

As they introduced her to Jesus Christ, she accepted and then told something really interesting. She said she had been sitting there drinking beer and when she saw the bus drive up with the name of the church plastered all over it she was ashamed to be drinking, so she started burying her beer cans in the sand!

See what an effective witness our bus is? She isn't pretty, she has an awful figure, her noise is terrible, her coloring is horrible, and she can't even talk, but I'll always love her with great affection from now on because God was able to use her in an interesting way.

THE REAL IMITATION

One Saturday as I was racing through work trying to get the end-of-the-week routine things done so I could get home and prepare for Sunday, my telephone rang. Answering it, I was disturbed to hear my teen-age daughter sobbing hysterically on the other end of the phone.

I pushed the panic button, as all mothers do, and said, "Honey, are you hurt?" She only sobbed louder when I said this, and I couldn't get any kind of an answer. My mind raced madly to all sorts of things that could have happened to her, or to the dog, or to the cat, or just any of the things that make a young girl's life revolve. And I kept saying, "Did something happen to the cat? Did something happen to the dog? Did you set fire to the kitchen? Did you fall down? Did you break something?"

It seemed to me I asked everything I could think of that would cause this crying. And each time all I got was a hysterical sob which I finally decided had to be a

No! I finally got quite stern and said, "Stop this crying right now and tell me what the trouble is!"

She finally blurted out, "I just read the Four Spiritual Laws to my friend and she accepted Christ, and I'm just like you, Mother; I had to cry!" And she broke out in tears again.

We had been having a "Week of Impact" at our church, as we reached out to bring Christ to individuals. And since Joan had gone along with me to the preparation meetings, she had learned that *anyone* can read the Four Spiritual Laws and introduce someone to Christ, so she thought she'd imitate the way she had heard me read the booklet and do the same thing.

And because I'm emotional and always involved with my entire heart and soul, upon occasion I have cried with a person who has just received Christ, and so she decided it was the accepted thing to do, and she cried, too! My heart thrilled to know that a thirteen-year-old who loved Christ could be used to win someone to him, and would then know the joy that only this can bring. I don't imply that bringing a person to Christ is always so simple. But she is, in my book a "real" imitation. Are you?

THE NEGATIVE WITNESS

In trying to show you just about every kind of witness you can possibly be, I have to mention the good old "Negative" Witness.

The day that Christ came into my life he brought me peace, joy, happiness, and a life that nothing else could match. In case you didn't read the testimony of my own life as written in *God Is Fabulous,* let me assure you there were a lot of little "shortcomings" or "sins" (if you want to call them that) in my life which slipped down the drain when Christ came in.

The other day I thought about something that hadn't occurred to me in ages. That was the fact that in my B.C. days I had quite a vocabulary of words which I used in a very interesting manner. As a matter of fact, the words must have been very, very interesting, because I used the same ones over and over again.

Now all I can say is I'm sure the words are still in my vocabulary somewhere, but they certainly got buried along the line because I haven't heard them since the day I became a Christian. However, my pastor who led me to Christ, never used a negative thought in introducing me to Christ, or I probably would have run so fast in the other direction he would have thought a tornado had just passed him up.

One time I heard someone say that when you become a Christian you have to take the ten things you *like to do the most* and *stop doing them,* and then take the ten things you *hate doing the most,* and *start doing them.* To make matters even worse, you have to pretend you *enjoy doing the things you really hate.* This to me is the Negative Witness. And I can't think of anyone who can run people in the opposite direction from Christ faster than the Negative Witness.

Have you ever listened to a "Christian" who said: "Boy, when you're a Christian, you *can't* smoke, you *can't* drink, you *can't* dance, you *can't* go to parties, you *can't* go to movies, you *can't* do anything that's fun anymore; but you're *saved!*" Who wants anything they *"can't"* do anything with! Not me!

I remember one time on a plane I listened to a woman tell me she would never become a Christian because someone had told her in addition to all the things

listed above, she had to wash feet as well! I can't think
of anything more uninviting to a non-Christian than to
be burdened with giving up all the worldly things they
enjoy, and then having to wash feet besides!

As I look at all the worldly things listed above, it
certainly seems to me I haven't had time to do any of
them for a long time, because they've all been replaced
with a life that is far more exciting and real than it ever
was when I indulged in all of those things. But I can
imagine the distaste with which I would have viewed
anyone who told me about all the things I had to "give
up."

It has been beautifully expressed that Christ doesn't
take away anything in your life; he merely replaces it
with another love. And this he certainly does! He replaces everything with a far greater thing than he ever
removes from your life. And what he gives you brings
far greater pleasure than any of the "worldly" things
could possibly bring. Yet how often we run ahead of
God and forget to remind ourselves that God's love will
show people the kind of life they are to lead, far better
than any set of rules and regulations we can establish!

The Negative Witness makes me wonder what happened to the joy that Christ promised, and the abundant
life he said was ours, because usually the Negative Witness wears a frown or a scowl and an "I disapprove of
you" look. This type of person doesn't allow God's love
to shine through, or even break through a tiny little
chink, because he's looking for the "no-no's" to tell you
about just so he can feel pious. (I imagine that's what
he thinks he feels like.) But I hope anyone who reads
this will look at his own Christian witness and see if he
belongs to the Negative Witness.

As I write this, I think of the man who carried a

heavy cross to Calvary, and whose nail-scarred hands show he died hanging on a cross to which he was nailed. And Christ did this for me! How could I possibly be negative in any way for someone who willingly took on himself the sins of all mankind that I might know eternal life? And God loves us so much that he allowed his Son to die for us. How could we ever think or mention a negative thought of any kind when we think of him?

THE POSITIVE WITNESS

Equally as bad in my opinion is the "Positive" Witness: the one who is always "right." Since a witness is "a person who can give a firsthand account of something," surely a witness who knows Christ "firsthand" can never show him except in great love. Doesn't it frizzle your nerves to have someone always assert himself as being 100 percent right? Paul says it so beautifully in Ephesians 4:15 when he says "But speaking the truth in *love*. . . ."

I have cringed upon occasion when I've heard someone with a "holier-than-thou" attitude talking to a new Christian, saying, "I *know* you couldn't possibly be a Christian, or you wouldn't smoke, drink," or whatever the person's particular fixation was at that moment. This is a crushing blow to the new Christian who is having problems anyway, without having someone be so positive he's not a Christian.

If you're still with me, *great!* Don't go away.

CHAPTER 3

AGE IS NO BARRIER

Sirs, what must I do to be saved? And they said, Believe on the Lord Jesus Christ, and thou shalt be saved, and thy house.—Acts 16:30b-31

Therefore many of them believed; also of honourable women which were Greeks, and of men, not a few.—Acts 17:12

I ALWAYS GET a kick out of people who give excuses for not witnessing and sharing the exciting news of Jesus Christ with their friends and relatives. And often I have been given statistics about the ages when people are most receptive to accepting Christ as their Savior. Sta-

29

tistics do bear out the fact that every Christian should concentrate on those who are in their early teens. This is when the ground is the most fertile, the most receptive, and the most searching.

But whenever I hear this I wonder where I would have been today if someone had not realized that age is no barrier to God. Becoming a Christian at the age of forty-eight or forty-nine, as I did, knocks a loop in most statistics and proves that *nothing* is impossible to God.

Recently I attended a Lay Institute for Evangelism put on by Campus Crusade for Christ. I listened to a dynamic Christian, Howard Ball, tell about how he, too, was obsessed with witnessing after he became a Christian. And yet the thing that meant most to him in life and the thing that he loved most in life he was unable to communicate to his own father.

I heard him tell how he as an individual had tried to persuade his dad to accept Christ. And how he finally realized he was not allowing God's love to show through him and communicate with his father. And how he was relying on himself and his desire to win another person to Christ instead of allowing the Holy Spirit to work through him. Suddenly the Holy Spirit convicted me concerning my own beloved mother-in-law.

Let me share with you a little about my mother-in-law (and don't cringe if you're a mother-in-law, because I have only good to say about my fabulous mother-in-law). She's a tiny little thing, only 4'10" tall, but a real woman of iron. She's eighty-six years of age at this writing, still does her own housework, and until the last year or two, did her own yardwork. She washes and irons, keeps her house immaculate, makes scrapbooks by the zillions, bakes homemade apple cakes for us, and leads a life that would kill the ordinary thirty-year-old housewife.

She finally gave up driving at the ripe old age of eighty-five by turning in her driver's license with the distinction of never having a traffic ticket. Grandma (as I've always called her) is as independent as they come. She doesn't intend for anyone to have to take care of her and she asks no favors from anyone. She remembers everyone's birthday, never forgets anniversaries.

She never has any aches or pains, and she can't stand anyone else who has them. Of course, I've seen her when it was obvious she was in pain from something or other, but she always fluffs it off with, "Oh, it's nothing —just this 'dang' old age, but I'll be all right tomorrow."

I wanted to share this intimate information about Grandma with you so you would know she's made of the "sterner stuff"—not a wishy-washy old woman. She'll take issue with you on any subject, political or otherwise, if she doesn't agree with you. And, of course, as you know, individuals with definite convictions of their own are often hard to convince otherwise.

However, when the Holy Spirit convicts me, there is no peace in my life until I have answered the call. As interested as I was in the Lay Institute, all I could feel was the tugging at my heart saying, "What's your excuse for Grandma?"

I had discussed Christianity in a fainthearted sort of way with Grandma. Because I have such great respect for her I didn't want to hurt her feelings by disagreeing with her. (Of course, apparently I didn't care whether she went to hell or not; I just didn't want to hurt her feelings while she was on this earth!) Grandma had a traumatic experience with "church" when she was a

31

very young girl. I really have no idea how correct this information is, but I only know the story as she has told it to me dozens of times.

It seems that as a little girl she had gone to Sunday school quite often. Never any one particular church, but various churches at various times. Her family always felt "you can be just as good outside of a church as inside because that's where the hypocrites are—inside," so there was just no need to attend church regularly. After all, if everyone lived as good a life as Grandma's family did, "this entire world would be a lot better off, and anyway, all the church wanted out of you was a lot of money."

When God reached down and really "grabbed" me for his kingdom, sharing this excitement and love with others became the supreme desire of my life. And yet when I talked with Grandma, I would always start off mildly with one or two little words, and then she would boom back at me, "Now you let me tell you what's wrong with churches!"

And then I would sit there for the next hour and listen to her tell me what was wrong with churches, because I didn't want to disagree with her or "hurt her feelings." I often wonder how God must have felt about me during those times when I deliberately held back the truth so as not to annoy Grandma.

We always ended such discussion with her saying, "And you just watch out for those buzzards. All they're after is your money and they'll take every cent they can get."

And then she'd add, "And I'll tell you how I know. These friends of mine had a baby who died. They were destitute, and had no money to pay a preacher for a funeral service or anything. But they wanted their baby buried from a church, and the undertaker took the little casket there, and the church wouldn't let him bring the body in because the parents didn't have any money." And then she'd smile and say, "See, all they want is money out of people."

I'd try to make some lame excuse that it does take money to run churches and we have to understand that the pastor has to be paid so that he and his family can live, and then this would bring on another tirade about how all the "preachers" took the money and lived high, wide, and handsome while the poor people starved trying to give them enough money to live on.

Finally, after a while, I just quit arguing with her at all, and finally my visits down there became further and further apart because I "knew" it was impossible to talk to her about the love of God and yet I couldn't stand to sit there and hear her say things I knew weren't the truth.

The tremendous tugging on my heart at the institute became a real pounding as the Holy Spirit spoke louder and louder to me concerning Grandma. And so I knew there was only one thing to do. At the intermission between the speaker and the classes I left the church. I had wanted so badly to stay for the smaller classes, but God said "Go!" And "GO" I did!

I almost ran out to my car obsessed with but one idea. And that was the fact that I had to override any objections Grandma might have concerning Christ— nope, I knew I had to let God's Holy Spirit use me that night as a channel for the words he wanted spoken. I was about twenty-five or thirty miles from where Grandma lives, and while I do not particularly enjoy night driving, *nothing* could have kept me from her home. And for the first time before going to visit her, I did what I should have done all along: I prayed! And I prayed! And I prayed!

Up until this night I had always negatively thought, "There's no use in my even trying to talk to her." But this night I prayed from the very depths of my soul, asking God over and over to prepare her heart, and asking him to use me in whatever way necessary to sow the seeds that needed to be sowed where Grandma was concerned.

I thought of the verse which says, "Watch and pray," and that's what I was doing. I was "watching" the cars zoom by me on U.S. No. 1 which is an extremely busy highway, and "praying" my heart out for the preparation of Grandma's heart. Because everything I do, I do with my heart and soul, I was so wound up from the exhilarating conversation with God that when I got to Grandma's home, I felt like I had been catapulted from my car as I opened the door. By this time it was ten o'clock at night, but I couldn't have cared less. All I knew was that God had spoken and that *this was the night!*

Grandma was so concerned when she saw who it was at that hour, and naturally thought something was wrong with my children. I assured her there was nothing wrong with my family, and that I was fine, and there was nothing wrong with me. But I also knew that God had sent me down there for one purpose, and that was not for ordinary chitchat, so I blurted out, "Grandma, do you know why I came down here tonight?" I didn't even pause. Since I had relinquished myself to God's will, he took over for me, and this is what happened:

I continued, "Grandma, you're eighty-six years old, and you're as healthy as can be, but at your age you could die tomorrow, and I *love you,* Grandma, and I don't want you to go to hell!"

And then she said, "Now let me tell you what's wrong with churches!"

And do you know what I heard myself say? I said, *"Oh, no you don't. Now you listen to me,* and I'll tell *you* what's wrong with churches, and I ought to know because I get in a lot more churches than you do." Then I continued: "But I'm not here to tell you what's wrong with churches tonight, Grandma, I'm only here to tell you the plain truth about Jesus Christ. I want you to know that God *loves* you, Grandma, and even at your age, he has a plan for your life."

And then I told her how I had been at the Lay Institute and how I had heard this man tell about his inability to share the love of his life with his beloved dad, and how he had finally won him to Christ. I told Grandma how much I loved her, and that the thought of her spending eternity in hell was too much for me to bear.

Moreover, I told her that, if she died and went to hell, her blood would be on my hands because I had failed to tell her the honest truth. And so I shared with her the exciting story of how God loved us so much that he sent "his only begotten Son, that whosoever believeth in him should not perish, but have everlasting life" (John 3:16b).

Sometimes it is impossible for us to believe that someone could have lived a whole lifetime and never heard the simple truth of the gospel. And yet it's true. I wonder how many times this same situation is repeated right here in the United States where we think that everyone has heard the gospel over and over again and yet never once have some heard it correctly in all its simplicity and love.

I reminded Grandma that God loved her so much that he wanted her to spend eternity with him, and when we realize how little time we actually spend on this earth in comparison with eternity, we realize that eternal life is far more important than temporal life.

I brought out the Four Spiritual Laws booklet, which is my favorite simplified way of soul winning, gave her a copy, and asked her to read along with me as I went through the various steps. When I got to the third law I very carefully went into the story of Nicodemus, and the necessity of being born again (or being born "from above"), the necessity for a spiritual birthday as well as a physical birthday. In other words, there comes that time when you must make the decision to accept Christ, and this establishes your spiritual birthday.

Watching her rebelliousness and "let me tell you what's wrong with churches" attitude, I saw her shoulders stiffen, and I prayed even harder as I read the laws to her. And then I saw and felt the mighty power of God again as I saw this eighty-six-year-old woman turn into a mass of jelly right in front of my eyes. I saw her shoulders drop. I saw a look in her eyes that I had never seen before. Then I saw her face light up, and I realized how we limit God many times.

Very simply I said "Grandma, is there any reason why you don't want to accept Christ right now?". . .

And she looked at me with a perfectly beautiful angelic look and said, "No, Honey, there isn't!"

Then I said, "All right, Grandma, on the next page there's a prayer of repentance, and because the light isn't so good, and because the print is little, I'll read it to you, and you say it after me as you invite Christ into your life."

Grandma grabbed my copy of the Four Spiritual

Laws out of my hand and said, "You'll do no such thing; I'll read them and pray *myself*." My cup of joy really overflowed as I heard her ask God to forgive her and as she invited Christ into her life.

Then I said, "Grandma, where is Christ right now?"

She said, "In my heart, where do you think?"

The Holy Spirit had done the job again! And the angels in heaven really must have rejoiced that night.

CHAPTER 4

... UNTIL DEATH US DO PART

> *Whosoever believeth that Jesus is the Christ is born of God. . . .*—1 John 5:1a

> *For whatsoever is born of God overcometh the world: and this is the victory that overcometh the world, even our faith.*—1 John 5:4

> *Blessed are the dead which die in the Lord from henceforth. . . .*—Revelation 14:13b

THE ELDERLY PATIENT had died—apparently of a heart attack. But because of an interesting medical history, an autopsy was made to determine the cause of death.

Several weeks later the medical examiner who did the autopsy was in a car with Dr. J. Lawton Smith, Miami,

Florida, world famous ophthalmologist and a mighty Christian warrior. The medical examiner was telling him about the elderly patient on whom he had performed an autopsy and he said, "This man was so unusual because he had on his face the most peaceful, serene look of anyone I have seen in the last ten or fifteen years."

Dr. Smith remembered having read in connection with aviation crashes that people carry certain expressions on their faces when they die. This is why it's possible to tell (if the faces aren't disfigured) whether or not a plane has had engine trouble. If the passengers *knew* there was going to be trouble, they had an expression of fear on their faces in death. In the case of an explosion or running into a mountain peak, there would be a mild, bland expression because of no foreknowledge of death.

Sometimes people die with a snarl on their faces. Sometimes with a smile. Sometimes with fear. Depending upon circumstances at the time of their death. But this man made even the medical examiner comment because of the beautiful, serene, peaceful look on his face.

And now that I've told you the end of the story, let me tell you how this particular story started. Dr. Smith had been treating an elderly patient for glaucoma and the patient, who was about ninety years old, was failing quite fast physically. Dr. Smith never misses an opportunity to witness, and, in talking to this man, felt that he was not a Christian. So he casually said, "When did you become a Christian?"

The man's countenance changed radically and he went completely away from the subject and told him how he had sung in the choir and how he had traveled with a choral group and how he had done this, and how he had done that. Then Dr. Smith said to him, "You know, if you should die tonight and the Lord should say to you, 'Why should I let you into heaven?' what would you say?"

The man's entire expresssion changed and he said, "I'd have to tell the Lord I don't know why he should let me in." Then he looked up and said he guessed he just didn't have the right answer.

Dr. Smith proceeded to share the Four Spiritual Laws with the man, who, after hearing the four laws and being confronted with Christ, when asked for a decision, backed away and said, "I want to think it over." At the ripe old age of ninety, he wanted "time to think it over." It doesn't make any difference how old we are actually, we never know when the Lord is going to say, "This night thy soul is required of thee." I honestly believe that at ninety I wouldn't waste much time thinking it over, but this was the case here.

Six weeks went by and one Saturday afternoon this man's wife called Dr. Smith and said her husband was feeling very poorly, having suffered a heart attack five days previously. Dr. Smith promised he would be right over to see her husband, even though their house was quite a distance for him to go.

After examining the patient, Dr. Smith talked to him. He said that he had been praying for him because he was so concerned about him and the fact that the last time he had said he didn't know the right answer as to why he should be allowed to enter heaven. Then Dr. Smith said, "I want to make sure before I leave today that you *know* the right answer."

Again he presented the Four Spiritual Laws, and this time the man accepted. Dr. Smith wanted the assurance that this man had truly been saved, so he said, "Do you

41

feel any different? Do you know where Christ is right now?"

And the old man smiled a beautiful smile and said, "I have just entered a new phase in my experience."

The following Tuesday he died. He had not been out of his apartment after accepting Christ and had seen no one, and therefore had been unable to witness in life, but the smile and the peace on his face gave him the opportunity he wanted.

He was witnessing to the medical examiner in death!

But Never Separated

Inside of me there burns a raging fire of desire to tell others about the excitement of knowing Christ, and the things he can do in a life, and of his promises of eternal life. In my particular life this is a consuming compulsion and it is impossible for me to do anything except my part in writing the 29th chapter of Acts. It would be easier to stop the flow of Niagara Falls than to shut me up where Christ is concerned, and because of this desire of my heart, the Christian Youth Movement, Alpha/Omega was born.

Many exciting things have happened in Alpha/Omega, but as I write this chapter, one particular incident comes vividly to my mind.

Some people have a "multitude ministry" and others have a "one-to-one" ministry. Still others are blessed with both types. At the end of each Alpha/Omega rally everyone present is challenged and given the opportunity to accept Christ after having seen his presence at work in some of the most exciting young people in the world. The only unfortunate part of a "multitude ministry" is that you don't always get to know the fruits of your efforts, but once in awhile something happens and you know the end result.

At the end of one of the Alpha/Omega rallies, a young boy made a decision for Christ. He then attended several of the meetings and was growing spiritually when it was discovered he had leukemia. It was the "galloping" kind, though I knew nothing about it until his sister came on stage (or I should say behind the stage) during a rally and told me that her brother was critically ill. Her mother wanted to know if I could come to the hospital quickly.

There's always a great decision to be made at a time like this. I sent a fervent prayer up to God, because I knew that to leave right then would be disastrous to a rally where there were more than 1,000 teen-agers in attendance. And yet a young boy hovered between life and death. I whispered to her that I would be there as soon as the rally was over. Ten minutes before the rally ended, the boy died.

It crushed me to know that I had been unable to be of comfort to someone who greatly needed comforting. But the next night while I was eating dinner a call came in for me with a message from the boy's mother. She very simply said, "Thank you. My son died with the smile of Jesus on his face, because you cared."

If nothing else is ever accomplished in Alpha/Omega, this one thing has made all my efforts worthwhile.

"I Stand at the Door and Knock . . ."

Witnessing is always one of the most exciting things in the Christian life because of the unusual things that happen. When you really let God use you it's amazing what can and does happen. Sometimes the things that

43

happen are hilarious; sometimes they're a little eerie; sometimes dangerous; sometimes unbelievable; always exciting; always thrilling, and certainly never dull.

My prayer-warrior friend, Barb, and I were out making calls one night, and we went to a home to visit a young couple. They had a little baby who was still awake when we got there, but the husband was out. Barb and I never talk in the car when we're out for the Lord, but we pray constantly asking God's Holy Spirit to really speak through us. So we went in, having decided by previous agreement it was my night to talk, and her night to be the back-up prayer-warrior.

We always try to find a common ground for talking to individuals we don't know, and before long we had discovered a mutual interest and were talking. It always intrigues me, when I'm visiting, to see when God is going to turn the situation around to the point where he gives me the "GO" signal on presenting Christ as a personal relationship.

We began discussing church, Jesus, the need for bringing up our children "in fear and admonition of the Lord." And I told of how I had not brought my oldest up in a Christian home and the subsequent problems I had. Even though I realize a Christian home does not always produce the perfect child, I had certainly discovered the odds are tremendously in your favor if your home is a Christian home (not of producing a "perfect" child, but of having fewer problems).

Both Barb and I gave short testimonies to what Christ had done in our lives, and then the "green light" flashed on. At this point I took out the Four Spiritual Laws booklets, gave one to Barbara, one to the hostess, and kept one for myself. From this point on, Barbara never talked, but just backed me up with prayer.

Everything went beautifully as we read the first three laws. The little boy was so quiet and attentive you would have thought he understood what we were doing, even though he was less than a year old. The mother was so attentive, so eager, so searching, so desirous.

And then I reached Law Four. To anyone who has ever witnessed, using this method, it's nothing new that you should be on the alert when you get to the fourth law.

During the reading of Law One, nothing happens.

During the reading of Law Two, nothing happens.

During the reading of Law Three, nothing happens.

But watch out for Satan himself during the reading of Law Four. I have seen everything happen at this point: dishes fall off the wall (from a plate rail). The telephone rings invariably. The doorbell rings incessantly. A jet plane roars overhead. The baby begins to cry. The meat begins to burn on the stove. The house catches fire, or somebody faints, or someone gets hurt—anything can happen, and usually does. But this night something happened which I've never had happen before or since (and I hope never does)!

I hope you can appreciate the reverent mood of all present when the Four Spiritual Laws are being presented. The Holy Spirit brings such a hushed atmosphere into a room at this time you almost know you can reach out and touch him.

I read the fourth law which says: "In Revelation 3:20, Christ is speaking and he says 'I stand at the door and knock . . .' "; and guess what happened! A knock came on the front door!

Barb is a real cute blonde and as I looked at her, her eyes were as big as saucers and she later said mine were, too! I'm sure both of our mouths fell open.

My back was to the door and it's a good thing, because I would have been scared to death to look at the door I think, because I knew it had to be either Christ himself or the devil. My heart was beating like a triphammer and I knew the door had opened because I heard it squeaking. Barb quickly bowed her head in prayer and I guess I just froze in my chair, waiting for I didn't know what.

All of this took only a matter of seconds, but I'm sure you can realize we felt it was an eternity. And do you have any idea how relieved we were when we saw it was the woman's husband who had come home?

God's Holy Spirit was so at work, however, that even this didn't break the spell. She handed him the baby and said, "Take him in the bedroom, quick." The husband grabbed the baby and left. Somehow God gave me the power to regain my composure; I continued reading the fourth law and she accepted Christ!

If your life is boring, I'd certainly suggest your asking God to use you in witnessing for him. I can really guarantee you action!

CHAPTER 5

NOT I WHO LIVES, BUT CHRIST

> *I am crucified with Christ: nevertheless I live; yet not I, but Christ liveth in me: and the life which I now live in the flesh I live by the faith of the Son of God, who loved me, and gave himself for me.*—
> Galatians 2:20

SINCE THE DAY Christ came into my life, he opened my mouth, and I haven't shut it since! How many times have I made this statement and how true it is. But the interesting thing is, in spite of the compelling force in my life to let everyone hear the exciting story of Jesus

Christ by letting God use me, every once in a while "I" manage to get in the way and then I really fall flat on my face.

It's so vital for the Christian to realize that God wants to use us, but he wants to use us "according to the working of his great might" (Ephesians 1:19). Often we run ahead of God and don't take advantage of his "great might."

Sometimes when you acquire a reputation as a "soul winner" others want to go along to see how you do it. And on occasion I have tried to show various people how "I do it." And talk about getting "hung up," I really get "hung up" when *I* try to do this.

God says in his Word that he will give us power to witness through his Holy Spirit, and sometimes we forget to utilize this.

One night an organization asked me to take one of its members with me on a "Go" call to show them how it could be done in a home, by a lay person. Naturally, my ego was flattered and I was glad to oblige. After all, wasn't I well known for being a "soul winner"? Let me say right here, I don't like the word "soul winner" because *none* of us is ever that. God adds to his kingdom daily, but we certainly do not. God uses us to sow the seeds, but for the actual new birth, only he can make this possible, and only through his power are new names written in the Book of Life.

But I guess we all get carried away once in a while (but thank heavens God knows how to humble me in a big hurry!). My ego had been flattered so greatly I really was a ball of fire and eager to show everyone how it was done. I could just visualize sitting back, basking in the excitement of hearing how *I* had "won" someone to Christ.

You will note that I have stressed the importance of prayer and the need for asking that God speak through his witness whenever making a call of this kind. Well this particular night I was *so* impressed with my own ability.

I chattered madly in the car explaining how to present everything so that the person visited would accept Christ, and then how to pray—but before you prayed, you might even cry a little because it would be a very exciting time and everyone would feel emotional, so if you wanted to cry, that would be all right, because I would probably cry, too.

I was so smug as I explained to my partner: "You will note that I don't have to actually use the booklet," because I had done this so many times I didn't need the book. "But it will be necessary for you to use the book until you are as familiar as I am with the procedure." I'm sure that God must have really been laughing at me that night as he prepared to pull the rug out from under me, because I forgot whose power and whose might would add to his kingdom.

We sailed bravely into the house, confident of some scalps on our belts, or souls on our halos, I don't know which. And after the usual amenities, I began "selling" Jesus Christ. I hope you will notice I use the word "selling" because that's exactly what I was doing.

I gave every reason in the book why this couple should accept Christ: "So you can have eternal life; so you won't have to go to hell; so you can have an abundant life here; so you can know the peace of God in your hearts (which I was beginning not to have at this point because I could see I was failing); so you can experience forgiveness of your sins." I went on and on trying

49

to "sell" them on the idea of inviting Christ into their hearts.

The man then said: "Christ is with me right now. He's sitting right on my shoulder this very minute." Somehow or other, I never did convince him that Christ was knocking at the door of his heart wanting entrance, and *certainly was not sitting on his shoulder*.

I did everything that night that was *humanly* possible to show that *I* could lead someone to Christ. But that was my problem. Everything that I did was "humanly" possible. But things that are "impossible to man, are possible with God," and I had not exercised the privilege of calling on God's Holy Spirit to use me. I had decided to use myself instead of being an open channel that God could use. And the little old thing called "ego" blocked God from using me that night.

Did I learn something that night? You bet I did. I said to myself, "How Great Thou Art *not!*" And I pray that I never again forget, "It is not I who lives, but Christ."

CHRIST IS THIN

Christ is interested in *every* area of life, including personal appearance. I have always been a *big* woman, and have always weighed too much. When my publishers told me they were going to send me to various places in conjunction with my first book, the Holy Spirit really convicted me about my weight.

I could just visualize myself waddling out onto a stage and making the grand statement, "Nothing is impossible to God,"—and then have some smart aleck kid in the front row say: "Oh, yeah, Fatso! How come you don't lose weight then?"

Knowing this would shoot holes in my whole testimony, I really prayed that Christ would show me the way to lose weight. I'm sure I have lost ten thousand pounds in my lifetime—and gained an equal number back, so I knew that by myself I'd be the usual mess. I completely gave the problem to God and asked him to show me what to do.

I'm hoping you will note that my reason for asking was for a furtherance of his work. And I didn't ask him to just melt the pounds off, I asked him to *show* me the way.

The next morning a woman, whom I had not seen for about six months, came into my office. And she had lost about sixty-five pounds. I gasped at the difference in her appearance, and before I uttered a sound, I silently *shouted* "Thank you Lord. So *soon?*"

And then I asked her to share with me how she had lost all the weight. She shared what had happened to her, and as I totally gave my problem to God, he really changed my eating habits *completely,* and while I eat *more* now, I weigh *less* than I have in years.

I'd like to share with you how the Lord gave me more opportunity to become the kind of woman he wanted me to be by showing me the way to a more attractive appearance. Did you know that your personal appearance can say as much about your happiness in life as anything else?

I want to be the best ambassador to the King that I can, and if improving my physical appearance helps me to be a better ambassador, then I'm all for it! And it's amazing what an exciting talking tool it is for Christ when people say to me, "What has happened to you? You look twenty years younger." They're really asking for it, aren't they? (And you'd better believe I really give it to them!)

I'd like to share with you how I lost weight and have been able to maintain the loss (without wrinkling up like an old prune).

BREAKFAST (don't let this turn you off. Just try it once):

> 1 slice of toast
> ¼ cup cottage cheese
> ½ cup fresh strawberries
> black coffee

I sweeten the berries with artificial sweetener. I no longer believe what I used to say to myself: "It leaves a nasty taste in my mouth. I just *have* to use sugar." I was kidding myself, because by trying several of the sweeteners, I discovered there's *at least one* that won't give me an aftertaste. Sometimes I slice apples on top of the cottage cheese and toast, put a little artificial sweetener on each apple slice, then sprinkle cinnamon on the whole thing and broil it under the broiler. I use oranges or any other fresh fruit in season, but I *do not eat the "forbidden fruits"* such as watermelon, bananas, cherries, grapes, papayas, or any kind of dried fruit.

As a change now and then, I have a whole orange (this stays with me longer than orange juice), one egg, and one piece of toast. I have discovered I'm not a very good dieter when I'm hungry, and the cottage cheese routine holds me from 7 in the morning until 2 or 3 in the afternoon, while I get the Devil's stomachache about 11 A.M. if I eat an egg in the morning. (You don't know what a Devil's stomachache is? That's hunger pangs!) Each day I also drink two glasses of skim milk. I buy powdered skim milk, mix it, and keep it cold in the refrigerator.

LUNCH: I cook any of the *"Christian"* vegetables which are:

cabbage	mushrooms
cauliflower	green peppers
bean sprouts	broccoli
asparagus	spinach
celery	squash

French-styled green beans

(Also "Christian" are lettuce, radishes and cucumbers, but I eat them raw, and not cooked!)

I cook any or all of these vegetables together, or sometimes I cook just one. Most of the time I make a huge pot, big enough for the entire week, bcause I use it many different ways. Seasoning is also very important: I use one of the dehydrated onion soup mixes to season with. And at the same time I put either chicken or beef bouillon in to season the vegetables. I'm a great mushroom lover, but I've discovered if I put too many mushrooms in, it will give me a "bad" taste in my mouth.

I take as large a helping of this as desired. On top, I put two ounces of any cheese which melts easily. I always heat the vegetables with the cheese cut up on the top, and when it's melted all the way through, I stick it under the broiler for a quick browning. It can be eaten with one piece of toast. For dessert, an orange or any other "Christian" fruit is suitable.

Sometimes I let the vegetables get cold, and eat them as a salad with a can of salmon on top, or a can of tuna fish. However, I eat no more than four ounces of the fish for lunch. I sprinkle vinegar on top of this and it's delicious! Or, two chopped hard-boiled eggs on top makes an interesting variety.

I'll have to share a funny story concerning "garbage"

(my term for this menu). I had always been so positive that my weight was caused by a glandular problem. Even though my daughter has the same weight problem I do, I *knew* it couldn't possibly be the food we ate. But when God provided the plan for weight reduction, I suggested to Joan that she go along with me on the eating plan. The first night I served the "garbage" she whined in typical teen-age tones: "I don't like the looks of that garbage!"

I love that daughter of mine, so I looked her right in the eye, grabbed the roll of fat around her middle, and said in the same whiny teen-age tone: "And I don't like the looks of all that fat!"

She never batted an eye, but said: "Gimme some of that garbage!" As of this writing, she's lost twenty-five pounds, and even more important, the teen-age pimples are gone.

SUPPER (There are vegetables which I refer to as "luke-warm Christian" vegetables. These include carrots, beets, peas, whole green beans, tomatoes, and such. I eat only a small quantity of these, but all I want of the "Christian" vegetables. I keep remembering, salad is really "Christian," but go light on the tomatoes! Most important of all, I find that for the supper meal it is most important not to eat anything that is "non-Christian" such as potatoes, gravy, whipped cream, pie, cake.):

Six to eight ounces of roast beef, chicken, fish, hamburger, or any lean meat works out well. But I have to stay away from "non-Christian" things like fat meat of any kind, pork or ham. (They're really not "non-Christian"—they're just plain fattening!) Any kind of fowl is fine: turkey, chicken, duck. I have quit frying things. This means that Southern fried chicken fans need to eat it another way in order to lose weight. I have come to think of foods such as corn, dried beans, macaroni as "non-Christian," and don't eat them. Potatoes and gravy are tools of the devil where the fat person is concerned.

Three to five fruits a day give me the natural sugar I need. I find this a real must because I have a "sweet tooth" and need sugar replacement. Personally I find oranges the best thing to curb the devil's "sweet tooth." I've been told that two glasses of skim milk a day will keep one from wrinkling as he "skinnies up." So I'm drinking it because I can't afford to take any chances at my age!

One night after I had spoken at a meeting where the air conditioning wasn't working, I was really warm, so I went over to the punch table and picked up a glass of fruit punch with ice cream in it. Just as I raised it to my lips, a voice behind me said, "That isn't very Christian, Mother!"

Now I ask you, could you drink it? Or would you have done what I did: put it down? Joan could have told me it was fattening and I wouldn't have worried, but we always refer to situations as being "non-Christian" and it really has an effect on me. Try it!

Ask your doctor first before you try this kind of diet, but mine says he's never seen me looking better, so may the Lord bless your *"Christian"* eating habits.

CHAPTER 6

"BY ALL MEANS . . ."

But now hath God set the members every one of them in the body as it hath pleased him.—1 Corinthians 12:18

And let us not be weary in well-doing: for in due season we shall reap, if we faint not.—Galatians 6:9

I THINK CHRIST is the most exciting person in the world because he thinks of the most interesting and unusual ways to use those who are willing to be used. And I often think of my favorite apostle, Paul, saying, "I am *all* things to *all* men, so that *some* might be saved."

57

One Saturday afternoon I was typing in my office—usually Saturday is not hectic like the rest of the week, and a good time to catch up on the unfinished details of the week—when a very unhappy looking young man came into my office and asked me to type a short letter for him. He wanted twenty copies of it because "I have to mail them out before twenty-four hours are up."

I said "I'll be glad to," but instead of the young man sitting down as customers usually do, he stood right by my typewriter as I started typing. I typed the first paragraph which went something like this:

"Mail this to twenty of your friends within twenty-four hours or bad luck will come to you. This is a *prayer* letter. *Good luck* will come to you if you make twenty copies of this letter, add your name to the bottom and mail it to twenty of your friends, but it must be done within twenty-four hours.

"Mr. ARQ mailed this letter and within twenty-four hours received $100,000 from an unknown friend who had died.

"Mr. ORZ laughed at this letter because he didn't believe in it, and within twenty-four hours his two children had been hurt in separate automobile accidents and were in different hospitals in intensive care with every bone in their bodies broken; his wife had drunk a bottle of poison thinking it was soda pop and was now dead, his mother was killed in a plane crash, his father was blinded in an explosion, and even his dog had gotten heartworm and was not expected to live. Mr. ORZ himself had stepped into an open manhole and had to have his leg amputated."

All of this had happened because he failed to send this ridiculous letter to twenty of his friends?

I had typed just about this much of the letter when I

looked up at this young man and said, "You don't really *believe* this garbage, do you?"

His reply came in on my God-given radar and he said, "Well, my luck has been so bad here lately I'm afraid not to send the letter out because of what might happen."

In case you're wondering what I call my "God-given radar," I'm speaking of an imaginary part of my anatomy which if it were real would have to look like two horns or a television antenna. And it's the most useful thing in the world when I'm talking to someone, because it picks up and sifts out a non-Christian's need for Christ. In other words, it's not a unique blessing in my life, and I *really don't have horns,* but it's the ability to *sense the need of an individual.* I sincerely believe this ability is given to every dedicated Christian.

As Christ heard the needs of his people, so he gives to his believers the ability to hear the needs of others. All we have to do is to be in such close communion with God that we are tuned in at all times. One of the things that I think helps me most in my Christian life was what my pastor once said to me: "I pray all the time. Even when I'm talking to an individual, I'm praying at the same time."

At that time I thought this would be a pretty neat trick if I could do it. And so I began asking God to teach me how to pray at all times, or to "pray without ceasing" while I ran a business, drove a car, taught Sunday school, talked to people.

I'm sure I could never have learned to do this by myself. But by asking God to show me how to keep in close touch with him at all times, I learned the secret of continual prayer. And this, I believe, is the secret of being tuned in to the needs of our fellowman. God

59

knows our needs before even we know them, and by constant communion with him, we, too, can know the needs of our fellowman.

My heart actually cried out when I realized the tremendous void in this young man's life. I stopped typing and asked, "Do you attend church?"

He said, "No, I used to, once in awhile. But I've had so many awful things happen to me, that I just don't go anymore because I think that God really hates me."

I silently prayed, "Well, thank you, Lord, you really do send me opportunities all the time, don't you?" I really asked God to make the young man's heart receptive to what I was going to say. Then I asked this young man if he believed in the Bible. He said that he believed in "some of the things."

I asked him if he believed the part which said that God loved him. He was very dubious about this because of his own personal life and all the problems he had.

We talked for about an hour as I told him what Christ had done in my life and how he had changed my life and had given me the most exciting, thrilling life in the world. I told him what Christ could do for him, and what Christ wanted to do for him because He said: "Come unto me all ye that . . . are heavy laden, and I will give you rest." (Matt. 11:28).

VARIED PATTERN

Witnessing and soul winning seem never to follow a definite pattern. The opportunity to witness and to sow the seeds in the soil of a human heart are never exactly the same twice. However, if we rely on the Holy Spirit, he will guide us safely through all of the opportunities he gives us.

I talked to this young man and discovered how unhappy he was, unhappy in his job, his personal life, his thwarted ambitions, just everything. There have been times in my Christian life when at this point the Holy Spirit gave me the "green light" to go ahead and present the plan of salvation and ask for an acceptance of Christ. But in this case, the Holy Spirit used a different approach.

We become overeager at times as "soul winning" Christians—and I'll tell you what I think about that word shortly—and we want to add "another notch to our belts." We go ahead without the "green light" of the Holy Spirit and by our own hard work try to "lead a soul to Christ." However, if you want to be a miserable flop, try it this way. Just try leading someone to Christ on your own. I dare you—*only if you want to find out what a lousy job you do by yourself.*

Even though I saw the great need in this young man's life, and even though I saw a searching heart, I felt the brakes applied by the Holy Spirit. And while we continued talking about God's love, I did not push the issue concerning the acceptance of Christ, nor did I even mention this except in a general way by casually saying "When I accepted Christ . . ."

I prayed earnestly for God's guidance in this young man's life and the next thing I knew I was inviting him to church with me the following morning. And he accepted! I put his name on my prayer list right then and there, and asked God to give him the courage to be there, and then I asked God to give my pastor the words that were needed in this young man's life.

In case you think that everyone who promises to attend church with me really means it, you'd better think again. I've had some people promise me on their "word

61

of honor" they would be there, and they haven't showed! So I've discovered that the "word of honor" of some people doesn't amount to very much.

After Sunday school the next morning I waited outside the church for my new friend. I prayed, I waited, I prayed, I waited, I prayed, I waited (I did this at the same time). Finally the organ began playing, so I knew I had to go inside the church. I was heartbroken because I felt that someone had been sent to me to help and somewhere or somehow I had flubbed it.

My heart was heavy as the service started, but before long God's presence was so near my heart was lifted on the wings of faith. As I listened to the sermon, all I could think of was how sad it was this young man had not come, because the sermon revolved around "Come unto me all ye who are heavy laden."

I went home, and as I was preparing Sunday dinner, my telephone rang. It was the young man with the "garbage" letter; he said, "I want to apologize for being late to church this morning. And then I want to apologize the second time for not staying and talking with you. But I think your pastor knew about me, because that sermon was meant just for me. I was so shaken up at the end of the service I had to leave."

Again God's Holy Spirit had taken over where there was a great need. We talked for about a half hour (or long enough to burn the potatoes—but who worries about things like that when a man's soul hangs in the balance?). He continued to ask questions concerning what happens when Christ comes into your heart. He said he thought it all sounded interesting, but he had so many problems in his life he couldn't consider accepting Christ until he got them straightened out.

Isn't it funny that so many want to straighten out

their problems *before* accepting Christ? And isn't it equally funny that no one *can* straighten them out before he accepts Christ? I often think if I had waited to solve my problems and get rid of my sins (whoops, there's that nasty word again) and straighten myself out before accepting Christ, even if I had lived a hundred years or more, I'd never have been able to do it. I often wonder if it's not a matter of pride because we really don't want Christ to know how awful we are, and we don't realize that he knows, even better than we do, how awful we really are!

I tried to explain to him that Christ wants us "just as we are." And because he wants us to know him in a personal way, he'll do all the changing in our lives that needs to be done.

The young man was completely intrigued with the fact that I talk constantly about Christ just as though he's actually alive. And he said he thought it was so interesting that I spoke of Christ as though he were right here all the time. He said "It really gives me goose pimples to hear you talk about him because I almost feel he's right here when you talk." Again, the Holy Spirit was working through an individual to reach another soul, because *I* could talk all night and never make Christ come alive to any person.

This young man continued to call me during the weeks that followed, seeking, asking, searching. And yet the Holy Spirit never gave me the "green light" to actually give him the opportunity to accept Christ. And I never went ahead on my own, because I've learned the hard way that this doesn't work.

One Sunday this young man asked if he could sit beside me during the church service. I was delighted because I knew this meant he was getting close to a decision for Christ. Again we heard an exciting sermon about what Christ can do in a life.

And as the invitation was extended at the end to those who wished to accept Christ, he began shaking so badly I honestly thought he was going to knock me through the wall of the church. Since we were sharing the hymnal, I had to reach for it with my other hand to steady it because he was shaking so badly. I whispered "Why don't you give your life to Christ right now?" And he hoarsely whispered, "No."

During the next week he continued to call me, asking question after question. Finally the following Saturday he called me three times during the afternoon. During the third call the Holy Spirit gave me the "green light." I said, "Do you realize you don't have to be in a church to accept Christ? I honestly feel from the urgency in your voice that you want to make your decision for Christ right now. Would you like for me to pray through with you right now?"

He almost yelled at me, "No!"

And as I fervently prayed for him, I said, "Please call me back if you'd like to accept Christ today. Don't turn your back on Christ if this is your hour of decision. Just remember I'll be at the telephone if you'd like to pray."

Please note that the Holy Spirit didn't encourage me to push him, because God never forces his will on any one, but he gave me compassion, love, and understanding to let the young man know I would be available when he made a decision.

I hung up and asked God to really let him know that the time was *now!* I had sensed the urgency in his voice and the need and the desire, and I didn't want him to quench God's plan for his life.

Within five minutes the phone rang again and a voice

said, "Can you pray with me *right now?* I can't go another minute without accepting Christ as my Savior and Lord."

My heart was really pounding as I thanked God for reminding my young friend that *now* was the time. I asked him if he was sure that this was the desire of his heart, and when he said, "Yes," I asked him to bow his head at the other end of the telephone line while I bowed mine. And for the next twenty minutes we prayed over the telephone as he asked God to forgive his sins and he accepted Christ.

"I am *all* things to *all* men, so that by *all* means, some might be saved." . . . even by the use of a modern day invention: the telephone.

You may be interested to know that the next morning when the invitation was given, this young man practically hurdled the pews to go forward and tell the world he had accepted Christ. He still has problems, but he's finding the answers and it's exciting to see him reaching out and bringing others to hear the gospel.

CHAPTER 7

THE UP-TIGHT DYNAMITE CHICK

*For we are his workmanship, created in
Christ Jesus unto good works, which God
hath before ordained that we should walk
in them.*—Ephesians 2:10

*I have planted, Apollos watered; but God
gave the increase.*—1 Corinthians 3:6

I OFTEN WONDER how I get myself in situations like I
do. But then I know that Christ puts me there, and always gives me the ability to get out of the situation as
well, and this next night was one of those "unusual"
ones.

I had been to a Christian coffeehouse under the

67

sponsorship of a experimental ministry, and the subject for the night was, by popular request, *"God."* Most of those who attended in the past belonged to a drug addicted crowd, and many openly admitted being LSD users, "pot" smokers, and the like.

It's so interesting to sit and watch during a dialogue at this type of coffeehouse, because it's so easy to pick out the marijuana users and the LSD takers by their various comments. And anyway, most of them make no attempt to conceal the fact of their addiction.

This particular night there were a lot of really rebellious college students there. The word had gone out that the subject was "God" and they were going to cut a lot of people down. Many times there will be so much conversation and rebuttal during an evening that not too much can be accomplished. But after the evening is over (usually around midnight), when the crowd goes outside, this is when the little groups form. And in each little group you can see a Christian excitedly talking, surrounded by a bunch of hippies, all trying to shoot holes in his theories.

This particular night the conversation in the coffeehouse had waxed hot and heavy about the impossibility of a living God. My heart ached for these young people who are so confused they refuse to admit the reality of a God to whom nothing is impossible. I literally wanted to take them in my arms and tell them to quit their searching, because the answer was so easy: just let God love them!

One young man in particular was the leader of the rebellion, and I really had a burden for him, so I asked God to use me somehow or other in this young man's life. He stood there smoking marijuana and defiantly dared anyone to even hint this was stupid.

We went outside and were standing on the street, and I said to him, "Do you really believe that God is nonexistent? Do you honestly think that the earth and everything in it just happened?"

This started a real tirade on his part and he said, "Listen, Babe, God didn't do nothin' for me. My old man made me, and everything I got in this world I got because of myself. I'm powerful, do you hear me? *powerful!*"

And while I'm not a pee wee in any sense of the word, he was a lot bigger than I am. And when he popped his fist into his open palm it made a big enough noise to kinda scare me, but not loud enough to keep me from loving some poor kid like this.

He was a little glassy-eyed from the marijuana but still had most of his faculties. So we verbally went back and forth for about two hours with his telling me that he was going to get everything he wanted out of life, *all by himself*. Nobody had ever given him anything, and nobody ever was! He said religion wasn't his "bag," but if I wanted to go around wearing my knees out praying, that was okay, but not for him.

I really have to have a sixth sense when talking with the hippie crowd because their language is so different from what I'm used to. But I have a good imagination and hope I know what they're talking about. He said, "The only thing I'm interested in, Babe, is the greens!" (Vegetables?) I hardly thought this was his "bag."

Then he expounded and said "greens" got you anything you wanted in life, but, "ya gotta have the greens." It finally dawned on me that he meant money, so I guess money was his "bag." He was studying to be a professional man—not because he liked what he was doing, but because he wanted the "greens."

He was so jittery I felt like giving him a tranquilizer, because he absolutely couldn't stand still. He looked like a tragic picture of a nervous wreck in the process of happening. Then he made the mistake of asking me what kind of tranquilizers I took because I was standing there so calmly.

I told him, "I always use God for a tranquilizer and get my energy from spiritual vitamins." This sort of surprised him, but he insisted I didn't know what living was until I had "heard a tree grow." He asked me if I had ever sat for hours trying to hear a tree grow. Somehow or other, this didn't send me, so I decided tree watching wasn't my "bag."

Finally I saw a breakthrough begin to occur. I asked him why he smoked "pot," and he replied, "So no one can hurt me! Marijuana makes me feel strong and I don't care what anyone says or does to me!"

I assured him that I had an armor that was so strong no one could hurt me and I had this without the bad side effects of marijuana. I told him how much God loved him, and how He had a plan for his life, if he would only give Him a chance.

He told me, "Knock it off. If I tell you I'm willing to try this way of life then you'll send a preacher around to see me and the preacher will make me go to church, and I wouldn't like that at all." Then he said, "And don't ask me what my name is, either. I won't tell you because you'll sic all the preachers on me, won't you?"

I said, "No, I wouldn't. But more than that, I wouldn't ask your name for anything, and I wouldn't even listen if you told me because if a minister happened to call on you, I wouldn't want you to think I had sent him."

I told him some of the things that Christ had done in

my life, how he had completely revolutionized it. I wanted him to know the same excitement and joy in Christ that I felt, and which anyone could feel, if he would only accept the love of God.

It was beginning to sprinkle by this time, but this is really unimportant when a man's soul hangs in the balance. So we continued our discussion in the rain. He said my approach was "heavy" (I thought he was talking about my weight). Then he said it was really "wet." And although it was raining a little harder, I assured him I wasn't wet, but he insisted I was. So I thought I'd just let him have his way, because one thing I have learned is *never to argue* with anyone while witnessing. This really "turns them off."

I noticed it was about 2 A.M. so I told him I had to go because I had an hour's drive home and had to get up for Sunday school and church the next morning. But I leaned over and dropped a Four Spiritual Laws booklet in his pocket, and said "Read that, will you please, tonight, before you go to bed. And then remember one thing! I'm going to put you on my prayer list, and you'd better watch out, 'cause you don't know what happens to people on my prayer list!"

He looked at me and smiled, and said, "Know what? You're an up-tight, dynamite chick. Will you come back next Saturday night?"

God had really begun his work again! That is the greatest compliment a hippie can pay you. I've since learned that being "heavy" and "wet" means I'm really "groovy." (Sometimes I can't even understand myself!)

Unfortunately the coffeehouse did not reopen again, because of a change of building ownership where it had been held. I had no way of contacting this young man. My heart ached for him. I continue to pray for him, knowing that at least the seeds have been sown. And I have done what Christ asked me to do. Who knows, maybe six months from now, maybe a year from now, maybe ten years from now this young man will accept Christ as his personal Savior because of something that was said to him by an "up-tight dynamite chick" standing outside a coffeehouse in the rain at 2 A.M. in the morning.

COFFEEHOUSE SPEAKER

Another coffeehouse incident was certainly unique in that the entertainment had been most unchristian. The audience was quite hostile as I was introduced. The management had previously announced that the author of *God Is Fabulous* was there as a special guest, and I could literally *feel* the resentment.

I almost chickened out of speaking that night because I had never felt such strong rebellion in my life. But I guess God lets this happen to me so that I'll really always remember to call on him. Just before I went on I said, "Lord, you'd really better get in here and do something, because I don't think they like us here."

And as always, when I scream madly for help (I was really praying with all my heart and soul), God heard my call. All of a sudden I remembred again that God is with me and that makes me a majority wherever I go. And so I said, "Lord, you'd better think of a really good opening for me, or we're sunk!"

Probably because of my age, the crowd didn't boo, but icicles were in the air after I was introduced. As I reached the microphone, God's Holy Spirit was really with me. He helped me start in an unusual way.

I said, "I'm not the usual type of entertainment. As a

matter of fact, I'm not even entertainment, but I'm going to share with you the most exciting person I've ever met—Jesus Christ!" You should have heard the groans! (Makes a speaker feel really loved and wanted, you know.)

Then I said, "I'm going to talk for thirty minutes, *but* if you don't want to listen, I'll give you exactly two minutes to leave, right now!"

With that bold statement, I just stopped except for sending silent prayers frantically to God. I stood there for two whole silent minutes which seemed like three hours. And would you like to know what happened? *Not one person left!* God had dropped a spiritual blanket down and enveloped each one there. You could have heard a pin drop for as long as I talked, sharing the excitement of Christ.

It was thrilling again to watch God work as I stepped out of the way and let him take over. The applause when I finished was unbelievable, not because of anything I had done, but because of what Christ was able to do through me as an open channel of his great love.

I personally wouldn't advocate using the approach of asking people to leave, unless God tells you to. I'm only trying in this book to show how every single situation in life presents a challenge to write a portion of that fabulous 29th chapter of Acts.

"God Gives the Increase"

Every opportunity to give Christ away is an exciting moment for the giver. Christ's presence is the only thing I know of which grows more and more as you give him away. Try it and see. The more you give him away, the more of him you have. And this continues on and on.

So if you want lots of Christ, try giving him away daily.

Someone told me recently how many promises Christ made in the Bible. I have forgotten the number but I know it was a tremendous number, and all I could think of was "How great! I hope to be able to claim all of them!"

When you think of all the various kinds of promises that Christ gave to us: the promise of supplying every need, the promise of eternal life, the promise of abundant life, the promise of spiritual light, the promise of salvation, the promise of power, the promise of prayer —I could go on indefinitely listing these promises— aren't we selfish when we refuse to share these with someone else? And aren't we more than selfish when we don't want anyone else sharing these promises with someone we're praying for?

Recently in my home we had an interesting experience. We had visiting us an out-of-town guest who was not a Christian. I have the kind of house where we always have room for one more—and we usually have three more instead of one. I've learned how to stretch food, stretch beds, stretch towels, stretch the budget, stretch everything, just because God gave me a tremendous love and a tremendous burden for people.

I have had as many as six extra teen-agers living in my house, and for a working woman this is quite a chore in case no one ever told you. One of my "adopted" children is a young man who is also my spiritual child and who really has a tremendous zeal for giving Christ away.

The young man who was a guest in our home was a searcher, we promptly discovered, and God gave me many opportunities to share Christ with him. He walked to my office every day and would ask me all kinds of searching questions. And I prayed that God would give me the right answers and use me to lead this one to Christ.

He was intrigued with the idea that we all talked about Christ all the time, and had prayer circles at night before we went to bed, and just publicly (around the table) prayed for the most impossible things concerning other people. Before the week was up he heard us thanking God for answering the prayers. He saw a "Way of Life" and heard a "Way of Life" that he had never quite thought possible before. He was amazed at the joy in our house as we all came home nightly and shared the exciting things that Christ had done during the day.

And even though I felt he was getting closer and closer to Christ, I never felt the "go" signal from God, so I just kept cultivating the soil. And then the night came. He had left on the table for me to read a letter which he was writing to a friend. He had forgotten one thing he had put in it, because he had written, "I guess God wants me to be one of Mrs. Gardner's Christians because I *know* I'm going to become a Christian before I come home."

The "green light" flashed! I put the letter down and went to the living room to actually introduce him to Christ. And do you know what happened? The Holy Spirit had descended upon the house and the "green light" apparently was flashing in every room and in every heart because, when I got to the living room, Rich, my spiritual child who lives with me, was reading the Third Spiritual Law.

I quickly sat down on the sofa and silently backed Rich up with prayer. And before my eyes I saw a thrilling example of "I have planted, Rich watered, and God made the increase." The thing that this brought home to me so vividly was God's plan wherein none of us should belong to Paul or Apollos, but *only* to Christ.

Here was someone whose heart God had prepared and yet did not let him belong to "Mrs. Gardner's Christians" because that's a nonexistent organization. We were thrilled that our friend became a brother in Christ and it was completely unimportant who actually led him to the final step. The only important thing was that he was a Christian.

Today he's witnessing madly because he knows what happens when you do. He knows it happened to him, and he also saw Christian love and cooperation. He knows that none of us had a desire for anything except to see him accept Christ.

CHAPTER 8

THE TIME IS NOW

Look unto me, and be ye saved, all the ends of the earth: for I am God, and there is none else.—Isaiah 45:22

Seek ye the Lord while he may be found, call ye upon him while he is near.—Isaiah 55:6

EVEN AS I write this book, the Lord continues daily to cross my path with people who are hungry for the truth! If you'll just discover how to use your built-in "radar," it's amazing how God can use you. Listen to what *I could have said*, and then listen to what *God* had me say to an individual who came into my office. (Let me explain that I have a display of *God Is Fabulous* in my office.)

Customer: "So you're an author, too!"

Me: "Yes, I wrote a book."

Not Me: "Not really, it's just a story that God wanted told, and he just happened to use me because I can type."

Customer: "It's an autobiography, isn't it?"

Me: "Yes, it tells what a fabulous life I have."

Not Me: "No, it's a story of Christ, and what he did in a life, and that life happened to be mine."

Customer: "I used to be able to write, but it seems to me like I'm dry. And I don't have the inspiration to write like you apparently do. It just seems to me that there's something missing in my life. And there's an awful emptiness there."

Me: "My goodness, isn't that a shame. Well, just keep trying and some one of these days you'll be able to write again. I certainly hope so."

Not Me: "Well, I once heard someone say that in every man there is a God-shaped vacuum that only God can fill. Maybe this is the problem in your life."

Customer: "Oh, no, I know all about Christ and I have studied the Bible and I know what *religion* does for you."

Me: "Well, that's good. Everyone should know about the Bible. And I think it's fine that you know a lot. Well, I wouldn't worry if I were you. I'd go to church, and before you know it, you'll be able to write again."

Not Me: "Would you mind if I asked you a personal question? You don't have to answer me if you

*don't want to, but I'm curious to know where you
have Christ. It's obvious to me that you have him
in your head, but I'm wondering if you have him
in your heart where he belongs."*

Customer: "You know, you've got me thinking, and I'm
wondering if you're not right in that my whole
problem is the fact that I have Christ in my head
and not in my heart."

Me: "That's probably your whole trouble, but I guess
there's nothing you can do about it."

*Not Me: "Would you mind if I shared a few exciting
things with you that have happened in my life
since I invited Christ to come in?"*

For the next few minutes I shared with her some of
the exciting recent events of my life, explaining each
time that because Christ was in my heart and living his
life *through* me, it was exciting to discover what God
wanted from my life. At that point she said, "Well, this
doesn't give you much choice, does it? It seems to me
like it's all cut and dried."

At this particular moment my pastor came in to pick
up the Sunday bulletins and I introduced him to this
customer. And in a way in which only the Lord can
lead, he picked up the conversation right where I left
off, and presented the Four Spiritual Laws to this
woman.

When he had finished, she looked at me and said,
"You know what? I feel that God led me into this office
this afternoon to talk to you, and then I think he had
your pastor come in right at this particular time, too."

Me: It's really a coincidence, isn't it?"

*Not Me: "It's interesting how the Lord works, isn't it?
And this answers the question that you just
asked, because while you were led to this office*

79

*this afternoon, and the Lord saw to it that my
pastor came in at just the right time, the decision
is still yours to make. He isn't going to force you
to accept him, but he has made himself available
to you through two of the instruments of his
work, but the choice is yours."*

Customer: "I choose to accept him as my Savior and
Lord."

And then while I bowed my head, she and my pastor
prayed. And she invited Christ into her life.

If you will look carefully at the foregoing conversation, you will see how easy it would have been for me to
say, "There wasn't anyone to witness to today." But if
you use your built-in radar, it's amazing how many
people the Lord will put in your path.

ANY WHERE, ANY TIME

And then there was the young girl whose life was
tragic. She had lost her husband and her two young
children in a horrible accident, and at twenty-three felt
as though nothing was worthwhile. She had taken the
insurance money and squandered it. Living high, wide
and handsome, she had blown $35,000 in a single year
and had absolutely nothing to show for it. When she realized it was gone—and even as she was spending it, she
realized what a complete mess she was making of her
life.

She had borrowed a car from a friend of my son's
wife, and had a blowout. She called my son and asked
him to come and fix it for her, and ultimately she ended
up at my house for dinner. This is not at all uncommon
or unusual, because I never really know how many I'm
going to have eating at my house. So I just fixed an

extra plate and I don't honestly remember how the conversation started, but I overheard her say to someone: "What I really need is a whole new life."

Instantly my "TV antenna" perked up its ears, so I just said: "That's interesting, because that's exactly what Christ offers you: a whole new life. As a matter of fact, in my Christmas letter two years ago I said that when Christ came into my life, nothing changed *except my whole life.*"

Now you might think this would have been the perfect moment to read the Four Spiritual Laws, but there was no "green light." So my "TV antenna" folded itself up and went back into normal position.

This young lady heard the conversation the rest of the evening, however. And I noticed that every night when I came home from work she happened to be there. I couldn't quite figure it out except I knew that the Lord had sent her for a reason and when he felt the time was right I would get the "GO" signal.

And sure enough, on a Sunday afternoon she was there, having visited my church in the morning. All the teen-agers who swarm all over my house were in swimming. Everyone was really having fun, but she seemed very quiet as she sat there on the porch.

The following night she appeared in my office and I asked her if she wanted to have dinner with us. She accepted. She had to go pick up something from her house, and was delayed so long I felt she must have changed her mind. So my daughter and I sat down to eat and were almost finished when she arrived.

When she came in, I kiddingly said, "Well, we prayed for an hour over the food, waiting for you, but then decided we'd have to go ahead and eat. But don't worry, we prayed for you, too!" It seemed to me this particular night I had so many prayer requests that prayer was really lengthy (because we have our prayer circle at the supper table when we're all together).

She said, "What did you pray for me?"

And I said, "That Christ would give you the whole new life you want." As I said this, the "green light" flashed, so I got two copies of the Four Spiritual Laws, one for her, and one for me, and I started reading.

The telephone must have rung at least ten times, but my daughter who was silently backing me up with prayer, each time answered the telephone saying I was not available at that moment.

When we finished, the young widow prayed to receive Christ. And my Lord became hers.

CHAPTER 9

TAKE OFF THE BLINDERS

Then the Spirit said unto Philip, Go near, and join thyself to this chariot.—Acts 8:29

And Jesus went forth, and saw a great multitude, and was moved with compassion toward them, and he healed their sick.—Matthew 14:14

As I WALK down any street, fly in any plane, shop in any store, work in any office, visit in any church, eat in any restaurant, engage in *any* activity, I find an opportunity to talk about Christ, an opportunity to fill the void in *someone's* life. I never start a day without asking God to prepare someone's heart for me to speak to. And I never start on any kind of trip—whether it's to the store or to another city—without asking God who he's prepared for me to talk to.

As I have written this book, which involves talking about Christ, I have tried to discover the reason some people talk about Christ, and some don't. After the knife-plunging in the first chapter about knowing Christ, I'll have to plunge another one in for a final thrust! Talking *about* Christ involves an awful lot of talking *to* God. Did you ever think of that? Maybe the reason we don't witness more is because we don't talk *to* God enough. And believe me, if we don't spend a good share of our time talking to God, all our labor will be just that—LABOR—and will be in vain.

On a recent trip I had left something in my hotel room and had to go back for it. Since I had some very important people waiting for me, I knew I had to hurry back. My hotel was about three blocks away from where I had the appointment, so I walked. And I honestly had to put "blinders" on—just like they do to a race horse—because I knew if I didn't, I'd get "sidetracked." And heaven only knows how long it would have been before I got back.

I literally had to hang my head and keep my eyes on the sidewalk so I couldn't see anyone for those few minutes, let alone see his need. But I wonder how many of us do this all the time? How many times have you ignored a real opportunity to talk about Christ because you were "too tired" or "afraid" or "just didn't want to"?

At a prayer group a young woman indicated a half-hearted desire to witness but said she couldn't get away from the house because of her six children. So we prayed the Lord would send her someone right to her house, because we knew how difficult it was for her to get out.

The next week when we asked her who the Lord had sent by, she sheepishly said: "I was watching a soap opera on television this week and a young salesman came to the door and started telling me his problems before trying to sell his product. I told him I was too busy then because I was watching a TV program. But after he left, I realized that God had answered your prayer and sent me someone to witness to, and I was 'too' busy watching television to take the time out to be concerned with him."

Ask yourself an honest question: If you were standing on the edge of a swimming pool, on the edge of a lake, or on the bank of a river, and you saw someone drowning, would you stand there and shake your head and say, "Tsk, tsk, isn't that awful? He's about to die!" Or would you do something about it? Or would you at least *try* to do something about it? I believe you would scream for help, or throw a lifeline in, or even jump in yourself if you were really brave, but I just know you wouldn't stand there shaking your head and watching a human being drowned, and do nothing but say, "Isn't that awful?"

Let's turn the situation around. What do you do when you have someone who is spiritually "dead" and with whom you're in contact constantly? Do you scream for help if you don't know what to do yourself? Do you throw him a lifeline? Or do you even dare to jump in after him and try to "save" him from spiritual death? Or do you just say, "Tsk, tsk, isn't that awful?" Well, if you're not out there witnessing for Christ, you're watching them die for eternity and doing nothing but saying, "Isn't that awful?" *It is awful.* It's awful that you're doing nothing about it!

Did you ever think about what you say when you go to the grocery store for your weekend shopping? Many salesclerks say, "Have a nice weekend." And I used to inanely reply, "Thank you, you too!" And one day the Holy Spirit convicted me of the fact I was throwing away a marvelous opportunity to witness, so I started replying: "Thank you, and you *really* will, if you go to church on Sunday." I'd like to challenge you to try this on someone. You've no idea of the interesting situations this has gotten me into and you've no idea of the witnessing opportunities this has given me.

My whole life sparkles since Christ put so much zip into it, and whenever someone asks me how I am, I always say: "Fabulous, but then I'm *always* fabulous!" And I'm certainly telling the truth because since Christ came into my life and I surrendered my *all* to him, I'm always *fabulous!* And you have no idea what an opportunity this gives me to witness. Every day people ask me how I can possibly always be *fabulous!* And then I just smile and say, "Oh, you just walked into something, did you know that?" And from then on I let the Holy Spirit do the job of witnessing for Christ.

I hope you've gathered from the things that I write that I have a great sense of humor. I think if all of us developed this, or encouraged this in ourselves, we'd be a lot better off in our witnessing for Christ! I hope you've noticed how humorous many of the situations are as I encountered someone to share Christ with, and what a boon this has been in the final development. I hope you are also aware of my extreme seriousness where the destiny of a soul is concerned.

I always give a copy of my book *God is Fabulous* to

someone on every plane trip I take. And it's always exciting to see who the Lord wants me to give it to.

Returning from a tour really tired, I assured God that if there was anyone he wanted me to talk to, I'd be glad to, but if it was all right with him, I'd just as soon "sack" out on the way home because I was exhausted! No one sat beside me on the plane, so I slept all the way home—well almost.

God always makes it easy for me to know who's to get the book, but on this trip I didn't get the "green light" on any of the stewardesses, so I just dozed.

The man in front of me had asked the stewardess at the beginning of the flight for two double scotch and sodas. He bolted them down with one swallow each, and promptly went to sleep, I guessed. I had not seen him or talked to him, but as we flew over Tampa I got the same nudging I had gotten from the beginning: the man ahead of me should get the book.

So I stuck a copy of the book between the seat and window as we approached Miami, saying, "I'm an author (great statement—one book to my credit) and I give a book away on each plane trip I take. Would you accept it?"

He couldn't see me through the little crack between the seat and the window, but I heard him say, "Yes, I'll be glad to." I pushed the book through to him. And as the plane landed soon after that, I wondered, "Lord, why him?"

And then I did a most unusual thing. I stood, waiting for the plane's door to open. He was still sitting. So I just rapped on his head with my fingers (don't we always rap on people's heads?) and in my most pious tone I said, "I hope it grabbeth you!" And I smiled.

He looked up at me, snarled, and said, "Not a chance —I'm an agnostic!"

I said, "How *exciting,* absolutely *great!* I knew that God had a reason for selecting *you* to have a copy of my book. Promise me you'll read it?"

He said: "Is it about you?" I said it was. He growled. "I wouldn't miss reading about a nut like you for anything!"

How exciting life is when we listen to what God says. I may never know what happened as a result of this encounter, but just think of the possibilities as God pointed out someone who really needed to read a story about a living God! *Take off the blinders and begin to live yourself!*

CHAPTER 10

LET'S GO—ALL THE WAY!

*If I will that he tarry till I come, what is
that to thee? follow thou me.*—John 21:22

*Finally, my brethren, be strong in the
Lord, and in the power of his might.*—
Ephesians 6:10

I HAVE ONE desire in life: to be an open channel for
God to use. I pray daily that my life will constantly be
completely open for his great and mighty love to flow
right through to reach others and start a fire for Jesus
Christ who is the consuming passion of my life. Then I
ask God to use me to fan the fire into a flame. Then I

ask him to use me to start another coal burning so that the first fire won't go out.

On an "enthusing" trip in Pennsylvania, I had a woman say to me, "I'll bet you never fail, do you?"

I really laughed, and said "Are you kidding?"

I'd like to use the last few minutes of your reading time to reassure you of one fact: It's not a sin never to win someone to Christ, *but it's a sin not to try!*

Try to think of your witnessing life as a cross, or I should say a series of crosses on the road of life.

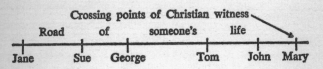

On the road shown six crosses are marked. The road represents a life: anyone's life. The crosses and the names indicate individuals who have witnessed to that person. Now each of them is vital to the final decision for Christ, but who deserves the most credit? Mary, who just accidentally happened to be on the spot when God added to his kingdom? Or Jane, who's the "low man on the totem pole," but who planted the original seed? Is any one of them any more important than any other? I don't think so. Our only responsibility is to do what Christ has commanded us to do: "Go, Man, GO!"

Maybe in the plan for your life God decided that you were a specialist at the third crossing point and so he planted you in a vital and key position for his work. We can't all be the quarterback who carries the ball and gets the touchdown. Maybe God just wants us to do our share along the line without ever getting any of the so-called "glory." Well, if that's your slot in life, *love it!*

That's why God put you there—to do your job, because it's as vital as any other person's on that road. That's why I believe it's not a sin never to win anyone to Christ, because maybe that isn't what God has called you for. But he has called you to witness for him, regardless of the outcome, and I haven't found one single excuse in the Bible for *anyone* not to witness.

I *know* why some don't witness! Do you? Do you believe the Bible and what it says? Then you'll have to believe what the book of Acts has to say about the power to witness. It simply says all we have to do is appropriate the power of the Holy Spirit, because the Holy Spirit will give us boldness to witness. It doesn't say that only a few will be bold. It says the Holy Spirit will so empower your life that you will be able to witness even to the ends of the earth. And it means *you* and *me,* every Christian. And I believe what the Bible says.

Throughout the experiences I've shared with you I've tried to emphasize two things: the necessity of being an open channel that God can use, and the necessity of prayer, asking God to prepare the hearts for you. You *must* be an open channel so the Holy Spirit can use you. And only God can make the increase, so it's necessary to ask him to prepare the hearts for you.

And don't always feel that "witnessing" is necessarily to those who are not Christian. Some of the most exciting "witnessing" I do is to Christians. You'll note I mentioned I was on an "enthusing" trip to Pennsylvania. When God first put the call on my life, I couldn't figure out what he wanted me to be. Then I discovered he didn't want me to be a preacher, or lecturer, or teacher, but he just wanted me to be an "enthuser."

Go, Man, Go!

Oftentimes in our Christian life we may run out of gas, or enthusiasm, or we need our spiritual batteries recharged to give us new Christian zest for witnessing. This is the exciting thing that God has called me for: to impart some of his zeal, or enthusiasm if you want to call it that, to those who have run down. So you see when you're up on a spiritually high level, you should share it with other Christians, because this is one of the most exciting types of witnessing there is. To revitalize a Christian is indeed a thrill. Try it sometime soon.

Is your Christianity alive? Is Christ such a compelling force in your life that you yourself have actually come alive? Does he really live his life through you? If he does, then I'm sure you're out on the battlefront witnessing. But if he doesn't I'd like to suggest that witnessing starts at home!

Make sure that you've witnessed to yourself so well that you're totally surrendered, so that you can be used however God wants to use you. Then remember that a heathen works from sun to sun, but the Christian's work is never done!

Knowing this, each Christian is challenged to "Go, Man, GO!" All the way!